TELL ME MORE! science

IN DISGUISE

How Animals Hide from Predators

by Ruth Owen

T0016542

RUBY TUESDAY BOOKS

Published in 2021 by Ruby Tuesday Books Ltd.

Consultant: Ross Piper
Designer: Emma Randall
Editor: Mark J. Sachner
Production: John Lingham

Photo credits:
FLPA: 4–5, 18–19; Nature Picture Library: 6–7, 10, 16–17; Ruby Tuesday Books: 22; Shutterstock: Cover, 1, 8–9, 11, 12 (bottom), 13, 14–15, 20–21; Superstock: 12 (top).

Library of Congress Control Number: 2020946817
Print (hardback) ISBN 978-1-78856-147-1
Print (paperback) ISBN 978-1-78856-148-8
eBook ISBN 978-1-78856-149-5

Printed and published in the United States of America
For further information including rights and permissions requests, please contact: **shan@rubytuesdaybooks.com**

Contents

Nothing to See Here!

Run ... hide ... fight back!

Animals avoid being eaten by **predators** in lots of ways.

Some animals have **camouflage** that helps them blend into their **habitat**.

A mossy frog

The mossy frog has green and brown skin that blends in with **moss** plants.

Some animals keep safe by looking like something else.

Fly pattern

Bird poop pattern

The pattern on this moth's wings looks like two flies feeding on a splat of bird poop!

Let's Talk

Why do you think the moth's pattern keeps it safe from predators?

(The answer is on page 24.)

Made of Moss?

Some kinds of stick **insects** hide from birds and other predators by looking like mossy twigs.

They are called moss **mimic** stick insects.

The pieces of fluffy green and brown moss on their bodies are **fake**.

They are actually made of hard stuff called chitin, and are part of the insect's exoskeleton.

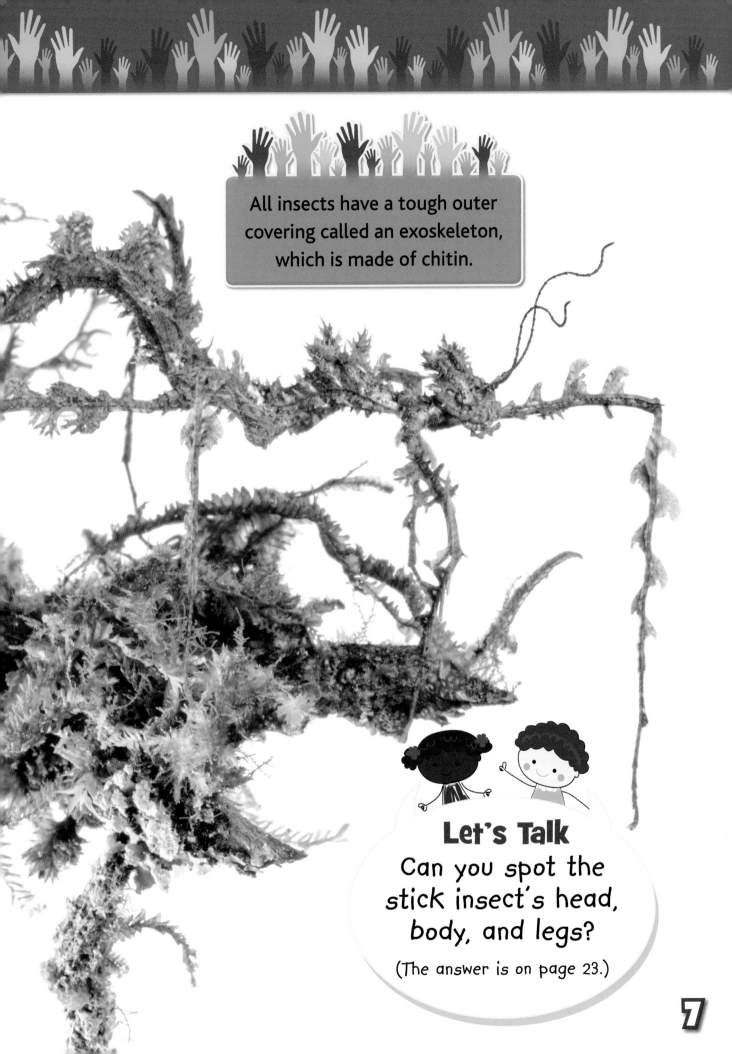

All insects have a tough outer covering called an exoskeleton, which is made of chitin.

Let's Talk

Can you spot the stick insect's head, body, and legs?

(The answer is on page 23.)

A Bug or a Leaf?

Leaf mimic katydids are masters of disguise.

Katydid

Some of these insects look like fresh green leaves.

Others look like dead brown leaves.

Katydid

Some leaf mimic katydids even have rough edges as if an animal has chewed on them!

Every katydid is **unique** with its own pattern or shape.

Let's Talk
Why do you think being unique helps keep katydids safe?
(The answer is on page 24.)

To stay safe, a leaf mimic katydid stands perfectly still. Then hungry predators, such as monkeys, think it's just a leaf and not a juicy snack.

Caterpillar Tricks

A looper moth caterpillar looks just like a twig.

It stands up straight and keeps still to trick predators.

A looper moth caterpillar holds onto a real twig with body parts called prolegs.

Head

Looper moth caterpillar

Real twig

Prolegs

Branch-like parts

A common baron butterfly caterpillar

This caterpillar has branch-like parts on its body.

When it keeps still on a leaf, these parts help it blend in.

Even the stripe on its body looks like part of the **vein** on the leaf.

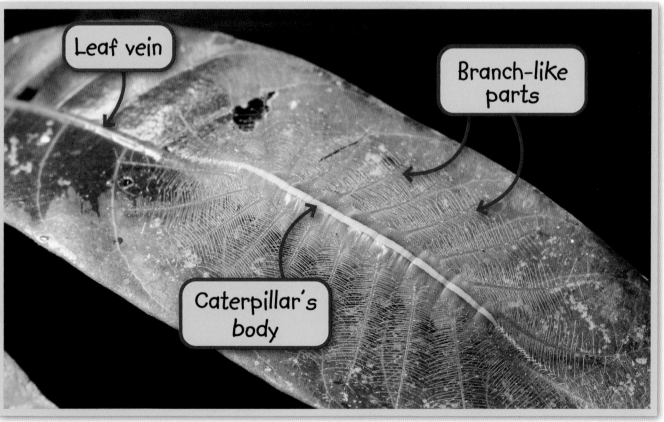

Leaf vein

Branch-like parts

Caterpillar's body

A Lump of Poop

Once a scarlet lily beetle **larva** hatches from its egg, it can become a bird's meal at any time.

Adult scarlet lily beetle

Egg

Larva

So how does the little insect stay safe?

The larva munches and munches on lily plant leaves.

The larva makes lots of poop that it sticks to its body.

Two larvae in disguise

Poop

Now the larva looks like a lump of bird poop.

This clever disguise keeps other animals from eating it.

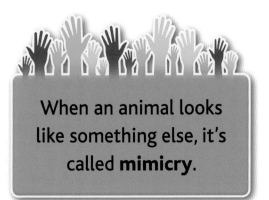

When an animal looks like something else, it's called **mimicry**.

What Gecko? Where?

In a **rain forest** tree on the island of Madagascar, a leaf-tailed gecko is resting.

The gecko flattens its body against the tree trunk.

There is fringe-like skin on the gecko's jaws and body.

Leaf-tailed gecko

Fringe-like skin

This fringe blurs its outline and helps it blend into tree bark.

The gecko's skin is such good camouflage, it almost disappears against the tree's bark!

By day, leaf-tailed geckos hide in trees. At night, these **nocturnal** lizards hunt for snails and insects.

A Feathery Disguise

At night, great potoo birds swoop through forests catching flying insects.

But by day, these birds are **prey** for monkeys and large falcons.

To avoid danger, a great potoo bird sits in a tree and stays completely still.

Its shape and colors make it look just like a broken branch.

A female great potoo bird lays a single egg on a branch. When her chick hatches, it acts like a broken branch, too.

A See-Through Frog

A glass frog's see-through body helps it blend in with its background.

Male glass frog

After a pair of glass frogs **mate**, the female lays her eggs on a leaf.

Mom hops away, but Dad stays to guard the eggs.

Eggs

Now, his yellow spots blend in with the eggs.

This keeps frog-eating predators from seeing him.

The frog's disguise also helps the eggs. When egg-eating wasps attack, they don't see Dad waiting nearby. The frog protects his eggs by kicking the wasps away with his back legs.

Hiding in Coral

There are many different kinds of **coral** in the ocean.

A type of coral known as gorgonian (gore-GO-nee-uhn) coral is home to tiny animals called **pygmy** seahorses.

Gorgonian coral

Pygmy seahorses have such good camouflage that no one knew they existed until 1969. A scientist accidentally discovered them when he was examining some gorgonian coral.

A pygmy seahorse is less than 1 inch (2.5 cm) long.

Its color and the tiny lumps on its body perfectly match its coral home.

Pygmy seahorse

Coral

Let's Investigate Camouflage

It might seem that the best camouflage for an animal that lives in a forest would be to have green fur or skin. But look at the three animals below. They all live in habitats where there are lots of trees and other plants.

Tiger   Jaguar   Giant panda

Gather Your Equipment:

- Printer paper
- Paints and paintbrushes
- Scissors
- A notebook and pen
- A camera or cell phone

Why do the animals have these fur patterns and colors? Let's investigate!

1 Begin by finding a shady place in a garden, park, or playground where there are plants with tall stems. Carefully observe the shadows in this spot.

2 Paint a picture of each of the animals. Your picture should almost fill a piece of printer paper. Cut out the pictures.

Which animal do you think will be the hardest to see when you hide it among the shady plants? Why? Record your prediction and ideas in your notebook.

3 One by one, place your animals in among the shady plants.

Is the animal's color or pattern good camouflage? Why? Record your observations.

4 If you can, take a photo of each animal hiding in its mini forest. Print out the photos and glue them into your notebook alongside your results.

Which of your animals was the most difficult to see? What do your results tell you about animal patterns and colors in forests?

ANSWER: How do animals' fur patterns and colors help them stay hidden in green forests! Stripes, spots, and patches of black and white fur can be good camouflage in a shady forest. These patterns break up an animal's outline and help it blend into areas of light and shade.

Glossary

camouflage
Colors, markings, or body parts that help an animal blend into its habitat.

coral
Living things that look a little like plants, but are made of tiny animals called coral polyps. The polyps join and live together.

fake
Not real.

habitat
The place where a living thing, such as a plant or animal, makes its home. Gardens, forests, and the ocean are all types of habitats.

insect
A tiny animal with six legs, a body in three parts, and an exoskeleton.

larva
The young form of an insect that hatches from an egg.

mate
To get together to produce young.

mimic
To act or look like something else.

mimicry
Looking or acting like something else to stay safe from predators or to trick prey.

moss
Tiny plants that often grow on rocks and logs. They look a little like a green carpet.

nocturnal
Only active at night. Nocturnal animals sleep during the day.

predator
An animal that hunts and eats other animals.

prey
An animal that is hunted by other animals for food.

pygmy
A word that is used to describe something that is smaller than normal.

rain forest
A thick forest of tall trees and other plants where lots of rain falls.

unique
One of a kind.

veins
Thin tubes that carry water through a plant's leaves. In a person or animal's body, veins carry blood.

Answer Page 7

Head

Index

Read More

Owen, Ruth. *Disgusting Animal Defenses (It's a Fact!)*. Minneapolis, MN: Ruby Tuesday Books (2014).

Owen, Ruth. *Wings, Paws, Scales, and Claws: Let's Investigate Animal Bodies (Get Started With STEM)*. Minneapolis, MN: Ruby Tuesday Books (2017).

Answers

Page 5:
Without its poop pattern, the moth might look tasty to a hungry bird or other predator. But most animals avoid eating poop, so the moth's disgusting disguise makes predators leave it alone.

Page 9:
The main predators of leaf mimic katydids are monkeys—and monkeys are smart! If every katydid had the same shape or color, monkeys would soon learn to spot katydids disguised as leaves. But if every katydid is unique, it's much harder for a monkey to figure out what is a real leaf and what is an insect in disguise.